It's a Cat's Life!

30 Original Cat Patterns
for Stained Glass

by
Robin Anderson
Sunny Brook Studio
www.sunnybrookstudio.com

VINEGAR HILL PRESS

Would You Like to Get These Patterns Electronically?

This collection is available as an "extended e-book" from Sunny Brook Studio. The extended package includes the complete book in PDF format, plus all patterns in both JPG and GlassEye formats. For ordering information, please visit:

http://www.sunnybrookstudio.com/books/Catgallery.shtml

You may also order individual electronic patterns sized to your specifications for just $2 per pattern. For details, please e-mail **Robin Anderson** at **rlandersn@suddenlink.net**. Please specify JPG or GlassEye.

Don't see your favorite breed here? Want a different pose? Sunny Brook Studio can create a custom design just for you. We specialize in creating beautiful, original, one-of-a-kind works of art in glass from photos of your cherished pet. Please e-mail **Robin Anderson** at **rlandersn@suddenlink.net** for a custom quote.

Visit our online gallery for more examples of our pet panels:

http://www.sunnybrookstudio.com/gallery1.shtml

Table of Contents

About the Author

Pets have been a part of my life for as long as I can remember—literally! The Anderson family had a long history of multiple dogs and cats; in particular, two Siamese cats, Coco and Saki, were constant companions in my childhood. (They're also the inspiration for several of the designs in this book!)

As soon as I returned from a year abroad as a graduate student, I adopted my own kitty companion, a tabby named Tatu. Since then, my home has never been "cat-less," hosting at least two, and often more, felines. I seem to be a magnet for stray cats, from Hamlet (an orange tom) to Warpaint (a long-haired calico), to blue-eyed Sinatra (the inspiration for "Season's Greetings"), to Ditch Kitty, who literally wandered up one day from the ditch. My house sometimes seems full to the brim with cats and dogs, who are each others' fondest companions.

Every day, cats fascinate me with their entertaining activities. Even eating and sleeping and staring out the window are done with style!

Another Anderson family tradition is "arts and crafts." Everyone in the family has had a finger or two in the arts. After dabbling in beading, ceramics, and dollhouse miniatures, I took a class in stained glass – and was hooked! I have been working in stained glass since 1998, and combining glass with my love of pets has seemed a match made in Heaven.

Since 2008, I have specialized in stained glass pet memorials, capturing the memories of beloved dogs, cats, horses, mules, and even a goat! I love working with glass, but even more, I love designing. I hope this book will be just one of many. It is the third in my series on pet

designs, the first two being *Best in Show: Purebred Dogs in Glass,* and *Best in Show: Puppy Class!*

Today, whether I'm in the studio working with glass, or in the office designing a new pattern, I'm usually accompanied by my two dogs and a cat or two. It's a family tradition!

This book is dedicated to Ms. Huggs, my French Chartreuse dowager kitty, who loves to put her paws on my shoulders and give me a hug. She has been my constant companion – and is the inspiration for the pattern "Basket Cat."

—Robin Anderson
Sunny Brook Studio

P.S. – Please drop by my "online studio" for a visit at http://www.sunnybrookstudio.com!

Tips for Designing Cats in Stained Glass

Glass Choices

Ask your stained glass retailer for help in finding glass as close as possible to the animal's coloring, but know that some colors are more difficult to achieve than others.

Tabby cats: There is no glass that will properly show the gradations of grey and brown stripes found on most tabby cats. You have a couple of options here:

- **Spectrum Glass** makes a couple of glasses that work fairly well for the grey/brown and black/grey of tabby coats: Spectrum 6011-85CC ("Hawkswing"), and SP 6009-8CC ("Thunderhead"). Both of these glasses vary enormously from sheet to sheet, so you may have to search to find one that comes closest to what you want. But the result can be a good base glass for the tabby.
- **Glass paint:** Once your panel is completely soldered and cleaned, but before you apply any polishing compound or cleaner, you can add some careful "striping" by using a black acrylic or enamel non-fired glass paint. Apply it with a tiny brush, like an eyeliner brush. Let the paint dry completely before doing your final polish and cleanup. If there is paint in the wrong place, or you don't like the effect, dry paint can be easily removed with the tip of a sharp Exacto knife. ("Nesta," shown here, was a light brown tabby. Her portrait was made using some of the lighter portions of sheets of SP 6011-85CC. The striping was added using black glass paint with a very fine brush.)

Black Cats: There are *lots* of black cats in this world, and a lot more that have at least some black on their markings! Unfortunately there is no transparent black glass, so there are only a couple of choices available:

- An opaque, solid black, such as Spectrum's SP1009, or Bullseye 0100. These glasses are available in smooth and water texture.
- A very dark charcoal gray cathedral glass such as Bullseye 1129 or Armstrong 10. Light will show through these glasses. A couple of textures and styles are available, such as a seedy glass.

It is entirely a matter of personal preference, but generally speaking, if you are doing the rest of the cat in cathedral glass, you will probably want to use the charcoal grays, but if you are using semi-opaque, opalescent, or translucent glass, the opaque black will look best.

Texture and direction: Many of the glasses used to portray animals have either a definite texture, such as water glass or rough roll, or a clear directionality of color flow, as in the wispy and streaky glasses. Use these to your advantage to create the illusion of a flowing or wavy coat by cutting your pieces to follow the direction that the coat flows. This is easy to see if you are using cathedral glass, but if you are using semi-opaques and translucents, it's a good idea to position your pattern pieces while the glass is on a light-box.

Cathedrals versus opalescent or semi-opaque glass: Obviously the choice is yours! Many folks prefer to use only one or the other. Also, the decision may be influenced by the color or texture choices available. For example, the best glass for the beautiful grey of a Scottish Fold or Chartreuse is nearly opaque glass.

Doing the cat itself in opals or semi-opaques and the background in cathedrals does make the eye focus first on the cat, essentially bringing it to the foreground and de-emphasizing the background.

Whether you choose cathedrals or opals for the cat, try not to mix them on the cat itself. If you are doing the cat in a streaky semi-opaque glass except for, say, the ears, which you do in a cathedral, it really confuses the eye of the beholder. If you are using the opaque black glass on the cat, your best results will be achieved by using opals for the rest of the animal. One exception! Do the eyes in a cathedral – it absolutely animates those eyes!

Faces and Feet

The most complex parts of any cat panel are the details in the face and the feet and toes. To portray most of this detail would involve impossibly small pieces of glass, so here's an alternative that works very well.

Foil overlays: You can do overlays on either the front side of the panel, or if you are truly ambitious, on both sides. If you opt to do both sides, you may well want to do your work with the panel on a light box so that you can line everything up correctly. This system works exceptionally well for showing the cat's toes, or the nostrils, or any other detail work you want to add.

- As you are cutting out pieces that require overlays, be sure that you save each pattern piece indicating where the overlay will be applied.
- Do the overlays after all the pieces have been foiled and are ready for soldering.
- Clean each piece for overlay thoroughly with a Q-tip and alcohol. Dry thoroughly. This needs to be done to remove all oils, fingerprints, chemicals, etc., so that the foil will adhere tightly.
- Cover the overlay area with copper foil tape. Use your fid or burnisher to rub vigorously to ensure a good grip. (Hint: your fingernail works well too, as does an old pencil with the lead broken off.) Be especially sure that the junction of the overlay tape and the edge-wrapping is well attached.
- Take your pattern piece and tape it over the overlay foil.
- Use a pushpin to outline the future overlay with a dotted line. Remember to designate *both* sides of the line you will be cutting out. Then, carefully remove the pattern piece.
- Use a sharp Exacto blade to "connect the dots" and cut out the overlay. *Very* carefully peel away all the excess tape, leaving the overlay. Then, take your fid, burnisher, pencil, etc., to again burnish the overlay.

Soldering your overlay: Considerable care needs to be given when applying your solder to these delicate overlays. When applying flux, don't "scrub" it on – use a light touch, and apply flux sparingly, with the brush running the same direction of your lines, not across them.

- Apply the solder carefully. Take a small bead on the iron and just touch it to the overlay. The solder will run along the copper by itself. Repeat as necessary to get your bead all the way over the overlay. Try using the corner of your soldering iron rather than the entire flat edge. Don't use too much solder! Be particularly sure that the solder covers the junction of the overlay and the edge wrapping to ensure a permanent attachment.
- Sometimes, in spite of your utmost care, the overlay will come loose, and the iron will lift it off. If this happens, clean the area again thoroughly and re-apply the overlay.

Painting: Once you have the overlays in place and soldered, you can use non-fired glass acrylic or enamel paint to fill in the areas inside the overlay as necessary, for example the pupils, or toenails. This system works particularly well for the eyes, where you have the pupil, iris, and corners of the eye. For the glass piece, you can use a brown glass, for example, and then fill in the black pupil and white or black corners. If you have a blue-eyed cat, a piece of cathedral blue of the proper color will give a very dramatic result!

It also works well if you are showing the foot pads, where trying to do it in individual glass pieces would be nearly impossible. If you want to show the toenails, just drop the solder onto the overlay. Then, for even more realism, you can use a bit of black patina for the nails. Or, if you have a white toenail, just use some paint applied directly to the solder.

- Clean the overlay piece carefully and thoroughly. Remember to use a light touch and to clean with strokes going the same direction of the overlay, not across it.
- Use the smallest paintbrush you can find, such as an eyeliner brush. These are available at any craft or art store. Remember to clean your brush thoroughly between colors and when you are finished. (These paints are water-soluble and clean easily.)
- If you make a mistake in painting, it is best to remove it right away rather than waiting for it to dry. Use the tip of an Exacto knife to remove the offending paint.
- Let the paint dry at least an hour before doing your final cleanup and polishing of the panel. Once dried, the paint is quite durable.

Whiskers. Let's face it – a cat's whiskers are among its most important features. Most of the patterns in this book portray a cat without whiskers, just to keep the patterns as simple as possible, but you may want to add whiskers to a pattern. There are several ways of doing this:

1. Add them to the pattern itself. Draw them in on your printout and then cut the pieces to fit. However, this is the most difficult of the methods, simply because it results in a *lot* of very small pieces around the head and neck, where pieces are already generally small.
2. Here's an easier way. First, assemble the entire panel, and do your first, tack-, soldering. Cut some thin strips of copper foil and attach them to the glass where you want your whiskers. Be sure that the panel is absolutely clean before you do this. I recommend that you clean the whole panel to remove the flux, and then clean the area where the foil overlays will be going again, this time with alcohol, and allow it to dry. Be sure to burnish the overlays thoroughly, especially where they are on the glass. Then, add your finishing solder lines and carefully add solder to the overlay lines. Use the corner of your soldering iron tip to apply solder to the overlays and be careful not to linger on them, as the iron's heat can pull the overlay off completely. If that happens, just re-clean the area and start over. The bead-soldering will help to keep those overlay lines attached firmly.
3. Another alternative, after the construction of the panel is complete and the tack soldering is done, is to cut some pre-tinned lengths of wire, preferably 20 gauge, and lay them where you want them, then tack-solder them to any intersecting foil lines. (If you are trying to hold them in place while you attach them, be sure to use a pair of needle-nose pliers or tweezers to hold the wires – they get hot!) Then add your finishing solder layer. The advantage of this method is that you do not have to worry about the whiskers pulling off the panel, as can happen with foil overlays, plus you can bend the wire any way that you want it to achieve the desired effect. The disadvantage is that the wires will probably stick out a bit at the ends, which will make cleaning the panel more difficult as they can snag on your cleaning cloth. You can resolve this problem by soldering each free end onto an existing lead (not overlay) line.

The Abominable Inside Curve...

You are likely to encounter a number of pieces with inside curves, especially when trying to portray long, wavy coats or tails. These also appear when working around the muzzle and eye areas of a cat's face. Inside curves are tricky to cut and break successfully, but certainly *not* impossible.

The number-one best solution to cutting inside curves is the diamond ring glass saw. If you can afford to add this piece of equipment to your glass workshop, it will pay for itself in terms of frustration *and* mis-broken pieces in no time! It is particularly helpful when you have that "this is the only piece of glass that will give me the results I want" piece, where an accidental break in that valuable piece means disaster. However, if the glass saw is just not in your budget, there are ways to cut inside curves

The "Sliver" Approach

Remember that glass naturally wants to break in a straight line. Remember also that it will usually follow a score that is creating a small, fragile piece before it follows the score for a bigger, more substantial piece. So, use this to your advantage.

- First, trace your pattern onto the glass. Do *not* cut the outside edges yet! Keep the overall piece as strong as possible. Score across the inside curve, not point-to-point, but slightly beyond the points. Go ahead and break off the excess.
- Now, score a sliver of glass from one end to the other of the curve, again, *not* ending at the point, but a bit beyond it. (Why? Because those points are very fragile, and the chance of breaking them off is really high. So, by going beyond the point, if *that* part accidentally breaks off, no harm is done.)
- A question I am always asked is "How big is a sliver?" The sliver needs to be a fraction of the whole curve, but it needs to be wide enough that your breaking pliers can get a good grip on both sides of the score. A quarter-inch width usually works well.
- Very carefully, start the run at one end of the score, with just enough pressure on your pliers to hear that little "snick" that means that the run has started. Repeat the procedure at the other end of your curve. Finally, use a bit more pressure on the first run to gently break off the sliver.
- Here's another hint that I have found hugely increases the chances of a successful inside curve break!: When you apply that final pressure to break off the sliver, *very* slightly apply a bit of twist from the wrist toward the outside edge of the piece. This will apply a bit more pressure on the sliver than on the piece itself, thus encouraging the score to run correctly. Remember, the glass usually wants to break off the most fragile piece, i.e., the sliver, first. Try it!
- Now, repeat this process with another sliver, and again as often as needed to get somewhere close to your original pattern line. Finally, score and break the other lines in the pattern, but remember, always score and break your inside curves first! There! You've done it!

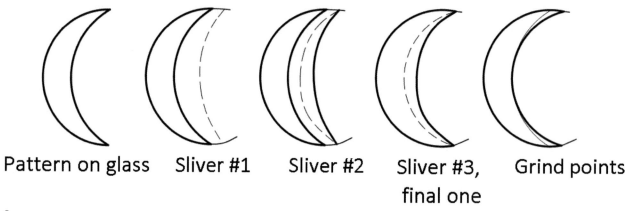

Pattern on glass   Sliver #1   Sliver #2   Sliver #3, final one   Grind points

The Grozing Method

A lot of artists like to chip away at an inside curve by scoring the glass and then using the grozing pliers to chip off the excess. If you are good at grozing, go for it! But the grozing method offers a significant potential to damage the piece at the pattern line, with scallops or chips or even undesirable runs. If you do groze your inside curve, don't try to groze right up to that pattern line. Stop far enough away from it that there is no damage, and then use the grinder to smooth and deepen the curve as needed.

The Grinder Method

This is the tried-and-true method for getting that inside curve. If you are working with a small piece, for example part of the muzzle, grinding is the best way to create your inside curve. The curve, and the piece itself, is too small to try using the sliver method. You can get grinder bits from your local stained glass retailer in a 1/4" and 1/8" diameter, which will make grinding these small pieces much easier!

But, depending on how deep and long your curve is, you may be spending a long time at the grinder, and wearing down your bit as well.

- Perhaps the best solution if you don't have a saw is to use the sliver method to get off the majority of the excess glass inside the curve. When you are close to having it complete, grind that last bit of glass away.
- If you are grinding the entire curve, again, do *not* follow that pattern line all the way out to the point of the curve. The pressure you are using to push the glass against the grinder bit can easily cause you to accidentally grind off that point. Save that final grinding of the point until the rest of the curve is done, and then address those points with a much more delicate pressure against the bit.

Foiling the Inside Curve

Foiling a deep inside curve can present a bit of a problem as well, because copper foil tape is not very elastic. When you put the tape along the edge of an inside curve and then burnish it down on both sides, the tape has a tendency to split at one or more points, depending on the depth of the curve. This will give a not-so-perfect solder line. However, if you "coax" the foil a bit, you can foil that curve without a single break! Here's how…

- When you lay the tape along the edge of the glass, don't pull on the tape. Let it lay down without any tension at all as you are pulling it off the spool. This will allow a bit of "give."
- Instead of using a fid or burnisher, use an old pencil without any lead at the tip – just the wooden part.
- Begin by lightly and gently burnishing the line where the tape bends to go down the sides of the glass piece. If you rub back and forth lightly, this warms the tape slightly and allows even more "give."
- Practice rolling the pencil between your thumb and forefinger. This also makes the process easier.
- Once the tape is bent over, use the pencil to push the tape to the glass, again using a firm but gentle touch and rolling the pencil back and forth. In most cases, the tape will go down without splitting, and you will have a nice, smooth line for your solder.
- Finally, go over the now-adhered tape with your regular fid or burnisher to be sure that it has a good grip on the glass. Mission accomplished! Remember, it's all about being patient, slow, and gentle.

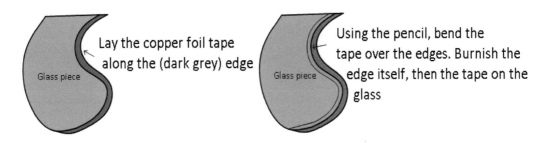

If, in spite of your best efforts, the tape does split, you can fix that too.

- Cut a piece of tape about ¾-inch long and burnish it down over the split, laying the tape perpendicular to the existing tape.
- Burnish it thoroughly.
- Then, take a sharp Exacto knife and carefully cut this tape so that the line is now smooth. Remember to do it on both sides.
- Finally, burnish it again, being careful not to dislodge the patch.

Making it Your Own Cat

Most of the patterns in this book are not breed-specific, with the exception of several Siamese (we had Siamese growing up, so they have a special place in my heart). This was intentional, so that it will be as easy as possible for you to make a design into a panel of *your* kitty.

If you are portraying a tabby cat, be sure to watch for the direction of the color flow in your glass. Before you cut your pattern pieces apart, put an arrow on each piece to indicate the flow, so that you can match it easily to the glass. Put your glass and pattern piece on a light box or in front of a light source when trying out different positions.

If your cat has different markings from those shown, you will simply have to adjust your pattern accordingly. Look at the differences between these two versions of the same pattern:

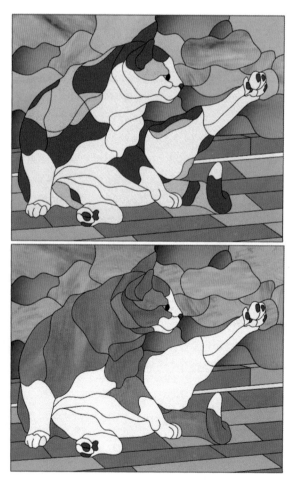

Here we have a calico kitty and a bi-colored kitty in the same pose. Note how lines are drawn to delineate the patches of color on the calico, but which are removed for the other cat. You can adapt your pattern in much the same way.

And now, enjoy the patterns – and make them your own!

Afternoon Nap

Basket Cat

Afternoon Nap

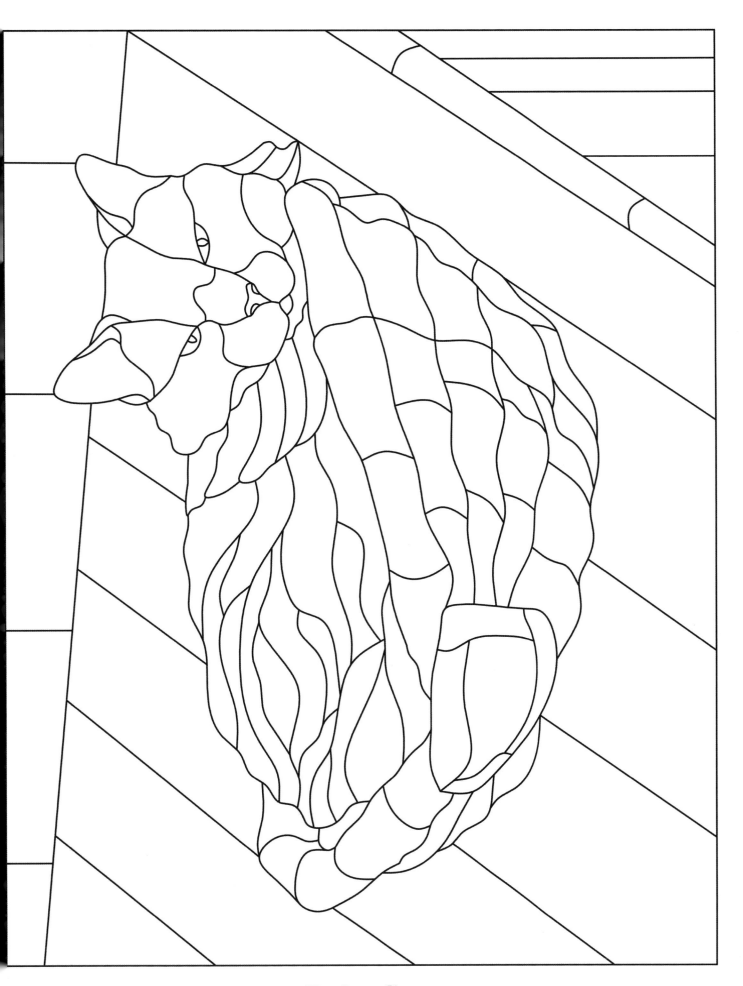

Basket Cat 13

Cat Burglar

This pattern is designed for the user to "dress up" to truly make their own. Find some costume jewelry (thrift shops and flea markets are great sources) and arrange it to fill the box. You could even give the cat a "collar" with a glittery necklace, or drape a piece over his paw.

The inset shows some ways to drape the jewelry over the sides of the box. Solder metal to lead lines in pieces that are metal-based (but be careful, as many pieces appear to be made of metal but are actually plastic). Use a spot of glue to make pieces hang properly. Do not solder to foil overlay lines, as this will pull the overlay off the panel. Arrange and "pile" jewelry in the box's interior to give it the look of a treasure chest.

The very narrow lines defining the box and window frame edges are done with foil overlays.

Cat Burglar

Christmas Present

Don't Bother Me!

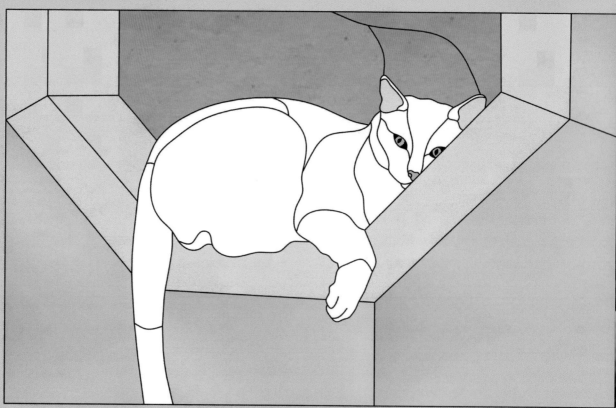

Christmas Present

Don't Bother Me!

Dreams in C

Gone Fishin'

Hanging On...

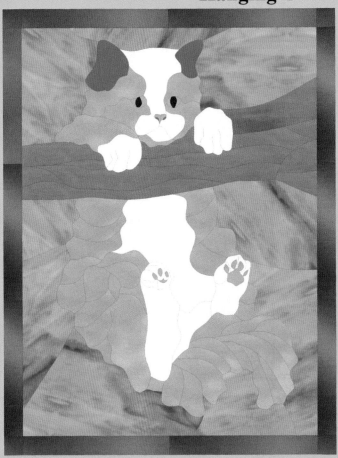

20   **Dreams in C**

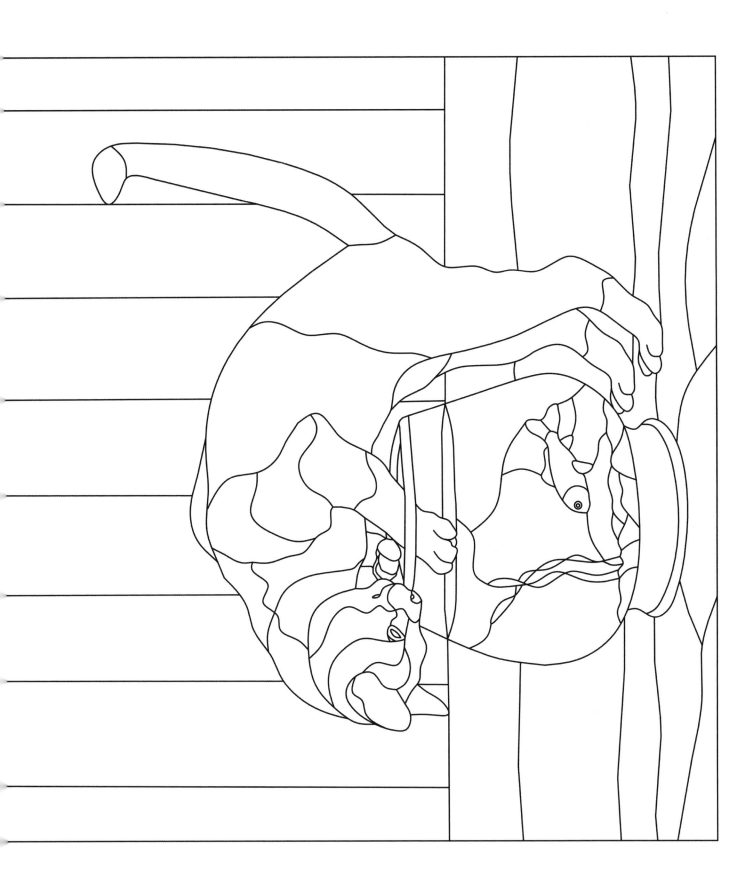

Gone Fishin'... 21

Hangin' On

Happy Halloween!

Honey Bunny

Happy Halloween!

Honey Bunny

Just Caught Dinner

Kissin' Cousins

Just Caught Supper!

27

Kissin' Cousins

Meditation Suncatcher (with and without sunbeam)

Literate Feline (with "old books" variation)

Literate Feline

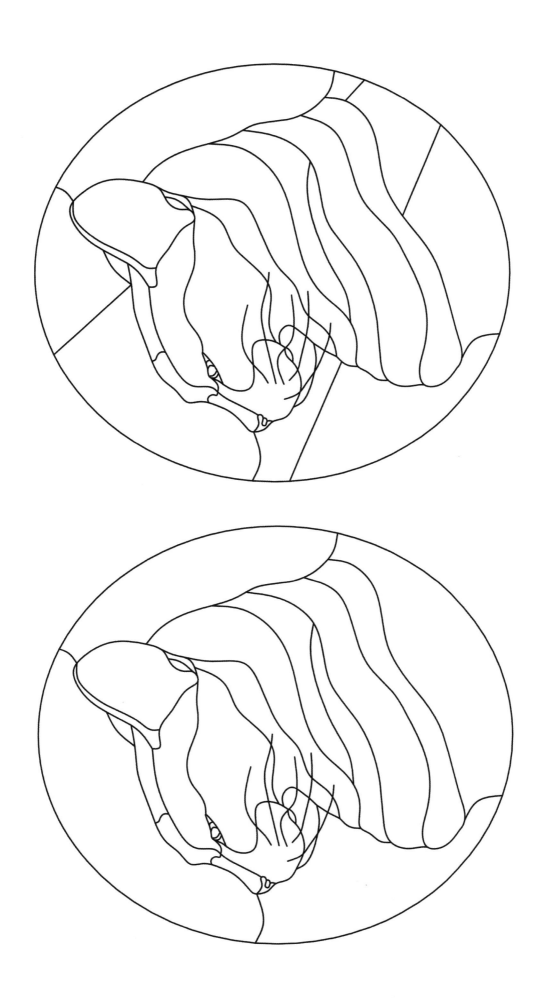

Meditation (with and without Sunbeam) 31

Morning Wash (calico and solid variations)

Morning Wash (Calico)

Morning Wash (Solid)

On the Fence

On a Roll

On a Roll

On the Fence

On the Lookout

Season's Greetings

Persian Yarn

On the Lookout

Persian Yarn

Season's Greetings!

Sun on My Face

That Looks Interesting!

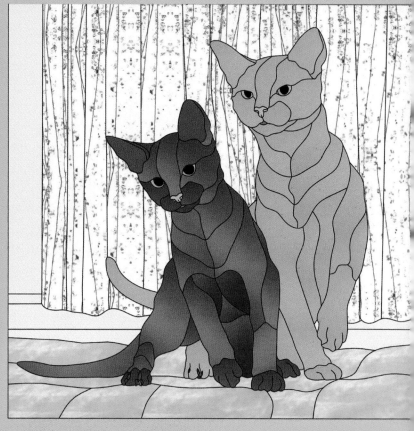

Sweethearts

Sun on My Face

Sweethearts

That Looks Interesting!

45

Tussle!

Two in a Typewriter Case

Tussle

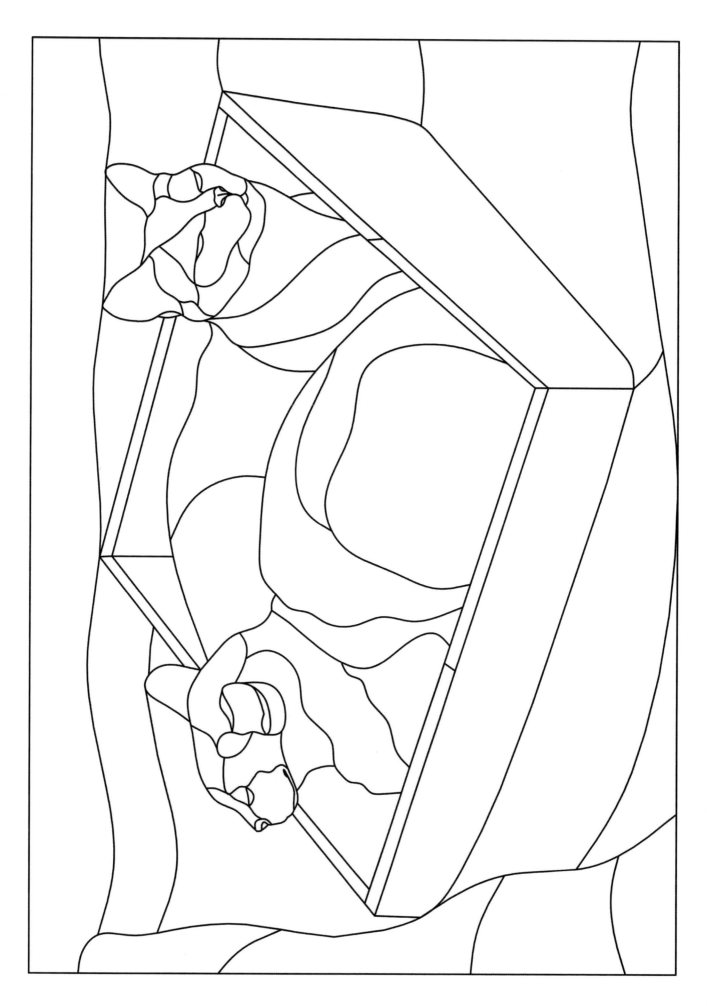

Two in a Typewriter Case

Up a Tree

Washbasin Cat

Up a Tree

Washbasin Cat 51

What's for Dinner?
(Seal Point & Lilac Point)

You Need a Bath!

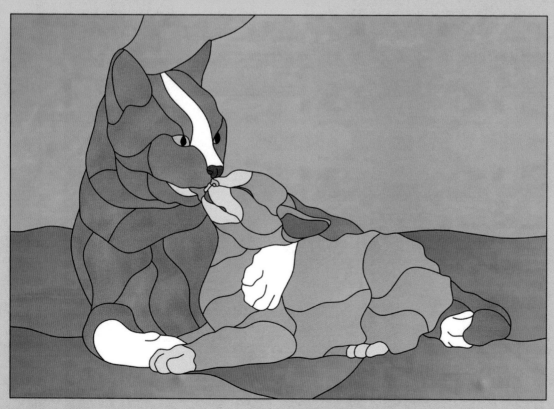

What's for Dinner? 53

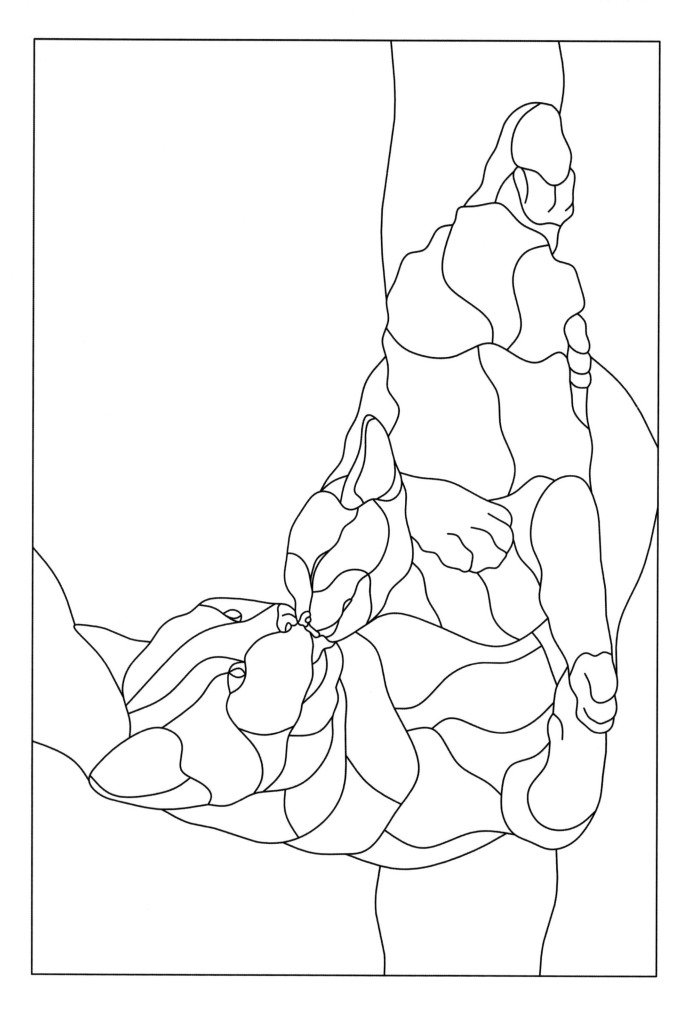

You Need a Bath!

Stained Glass Pattern Books by Robin Anderson:

Best in Show! Purebred Dogs in Glass
35 Original Patterns Representing the 7 AKC Groups

Available from your distributor or Amazon.com
For a preview, or information on how to order the *extended e-book* (which includes all patterns in JPG and GlassEye format), visit
http://www.sunnybrookstudio.com/books/BISgallery.shtml

Best in Show – Puppy Class!
28 Original Purebred Puppy Patterns

Available from your distributor or Amazon.com
For a preview, or information on how to order the *extended e-book* (which includes all patterns in JPG and GlassEye format), visit
http://www.sunnybrookstudio.com/books/Puppygallery.shtml

It's a Cat's Life!
30 Original Stained Glass Cat Patterns

Available from your distributor or Amazon.com
For a preview, or information on how to order the *extended e-book* (which includes all patterns in JPG and GlassEye format), visit
http://www.sunnybrookstudio.com/books/Catgallery.shtml

Made in the USA
Charleston, SC
29 October 2015